IT'S ALL ABOUT...

DOGS AND

PUPPIES

First published 2018 by Kingfisher
This edition published in 2021 by Kingfisher
an imprint of Macmillan Children's Books
The Smithson, 6 Briset Street, London, EC1M 5NR
Associated companies throughout the world
www.panmacmillan.com

Series editor: Sarah Snashall
Series design: Anthony Hannant and Laura Hall
Illustrations: Laura Hall
Written by Sarah Snashall

ISBN: 978-0-7534-4662-1

Copyright © Macmillan Publishers International Ltd 2018, 2021

9 8 7 6 5 4 3 2 1
1TR/0421/WKT/UG/128MA

EU representative: Macmillan Publishers Ireland Limited, Mallard Lodge,
Lansdowne Village, Dublin 4

A CIP catalogue record for this book is available from the British Library.

Printed in China

Picture credits
The Publisher would like to thank the following for permission to reproduce their material.
Top = t; Bottom = b; Centre = c; Left = l; Right = r
Cover iStock/Phonlamal Photo, back cover iStock/Sensor spot; pages 2–3, 30–31 iStock/
dageldog; 4 iStock/animalinfo; 4–5b iStock/MirasWonderland; 5t iStock/alexei_tm;
6b iStock/TeoLazarev; 6r iStock/Diyanski; 7t iStock/Eriklam; 7cl iStock/anna-av;
7b Shutterstock/Melounix; 8 iStock/Himagine; 9t Shutterstock/Natalia V Guseva; 9c Getty/
Auscape; 10–11 iStock/GlobalP; 11b iStock/igorr1; 12 iStock/LexitheMonster; 13t iStock/
EcoPic; 13b iStock/alvarez; 14 iStock/ventdusud; 15t iStock/cyclonphoto; 15b Alamy/Edwin
Remsburg; 16 Alamy/615 collection; 17t Alamy/tony french; 17b Alamy/SPUTNIK; 18 Alamy/
Classic Image; 19 iStock/fotofrankyat; 19br iStock/rohappy; 20 iStock/suriyasilsaksom;
21t iStock/crisserbug; 21c Alamy/JuniorsBildarchive GmbH; 21b Alamy/DK; 22 iStock/
wundervisuals; 23t Rex/Shutterstock/Virginamerica; 23c Shutterstock/otsphoto;
23b iStock/artpipi; 24 iStock/mato181; 25t iStock/Astakhova; 25b iStock/KateDobies;
26 iStock/kali9; 27t iStock/s5iztok; 27b iStock/Chuckee; 28 iStock/f8grapher;
29t iStock/lurlisokolov; 29b iStock/Sladic.

Front cover: An excited terrier puppy runs through grass.

CONTENTS

We love dogs!

Dogs have been living with humans for at least 10,000 years. For thousands of years, dogs helped people hunt for food. Today, most dogs are pets, though many work as sheep dogs, police dogs and guide dogs.

Dogs come in many different shapes, sizes and colour patterns.

Dogs are loyal and intelligent animals; they are playful and affectionate.

Big and small

All domestic dogs belong to one species of dog. But over thousands of years hundreds of very different-looking breeds of dog have developed.

We organize dog breeds into seven groups:
Working dogs
Terriers
Hounds
Gundogs
Utility dogs
Pastoral dogs
Toy dogs

The fast Borzoi was bred to hunt wolves.

English setters have a long, speckled coat.

The Great Dane is massive compared to the tiny Chihuahua.

Corgis are a favourite breed of Queen Elizabeth II.

Bull terriers have an egg-shaped face and triangular-shaped eyes.

7

All shapes and sizes

The biggest dog breed is the Great Dane; the smallest is the Chihuahua. The Komondor has the strangest hair; the Xoloitzcuintli (say *showlo-its-kwint-lee*) has no hair at all on its body.

Fastest dog: Greyhound
Longest hair: Komondor and Afghan Hound
Largest dog: Great Dane
Smallest dog: Chihuahua
Smartest dog: Border Collie

A greyhound is the fastest dog. It can run at 70 kilometres per hour.

The Bedlington terrier's curly coat makes it look like a lamb.

The Xoloitzcuintli only has hair on its head.

The Border Collie is one of the most intelligent dogs.

Strong and lean

The domestic dog is a cousin of the grey wolf. With its strong legs and lean body, the dog is still a hunting animal.

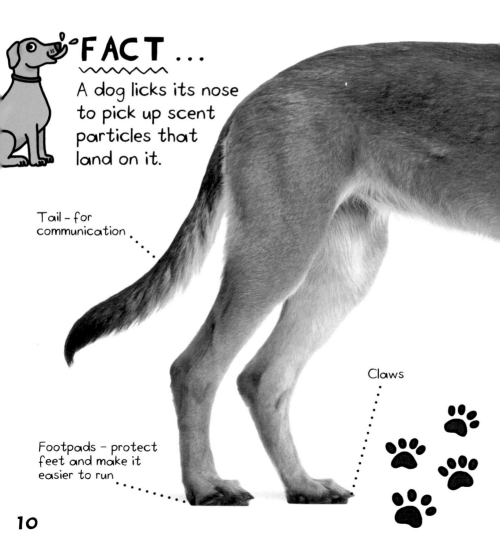

FACT ...

A dog licks its nose to pick up scent particles that land on it.

Tail – for communication

Claws

Footpads – protect feet and make it easier to run

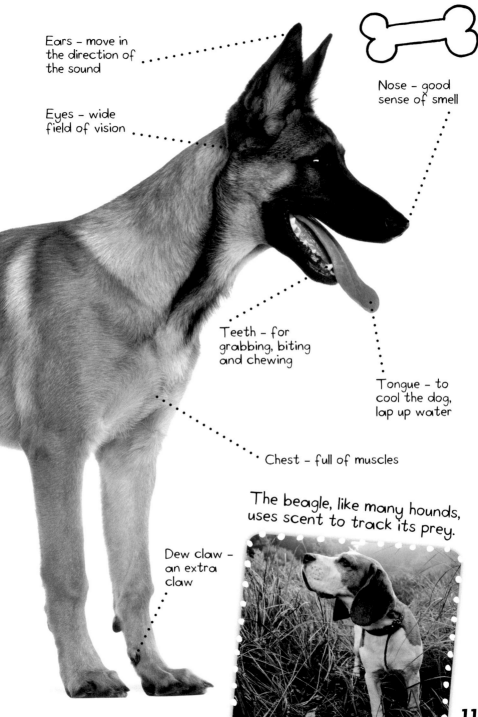

Ears - move in the direction of the sound

Nose - good sense of smell

Eyes - wide field of vision

Teeth - for grabbing, biting and chewing

Tongue - to cool the dog, lap up water

Chest - full of muscles

Dew claw - an extra claw

The beagle, like many hounds, uses scent to track its prey.

Hunters and chasers

Gundogs, hounds and terriers are bred for tracking and hunting animals. They have stamina and speed and strong hunting instincts. As pets, they need lots of exercise.

When a pointer detects prey it freezes and 'points' with its nose.

SPOTLIGHT: Mick the Miller

Famous for: first sporting super star who won 51 of his 68 races

Breed: greyhound

Owned by: Father Martin Brophy, Ireland

Once hunting dogs in Ancient Egypt, greyhounds are now famous for being racing dogs.

FACT...

Dalmatians were trained to run alongside stagecoaches to protect them from highwaymen.

Herders and workers

Dogs are intelligent and can be trained to work for us. Herding dogs guard and herd sheep and cattle. Working dogs guard houses and pull sledges. Service dogs help people who have limited sight, hearing or difficulty in getting around.

Sledge dog teams follow commands to turn left or right.

FACT ...

In 1925, twenty sledge dog teams travelled 1085 kilometres in relay in five and a half days. They travelled from Nenana to Nome in Alaska, USA to deliver life-saving medicine.

Guide dogs are trained from being puppies to help people with little or no eyesight move around safely.

Clever Border Collies herd a flock of sheep into a pen, or move them from field to field.

A dangerous job

Labrador retrievers and German shepherd dogs are strong and quick to learn. Well-trained dogs support the police, search for people after a disaster or work as guard dogs. Military dogs can find explosives and track enemies.

Military dogs sometimes wear special goggles to protect their eyes.

This search and rescue dog is trained to jump out of a helicopter to rescue people who are drowning.

SPOTLIGHT: Veterok and Ugolyok

Famous for:	the longest spaceflight made by dogs – 22 days!
Breed:	mixed
Owned by:	Russian Space Programme

Surviving the cold

Some working dogs have a thick double layer of fur. They work in cold places in the far north of the world, pulling sledges, hunting elk, saving lives and exploring.

Norwegian explorer Roald Amundsen took teams of Greenland dogs on his 1911 expedition to the South Pole.

Famous for: rescuing 40 people who became lost in the Alps

Breed: St Bernard

Owner: monks in Switzerland

FACT ...

St Bernard rescue dogs were trained to lick the people they found until they were warm.

Samoyeds have a thick double coat so they can survive very low temperatures.

Puppies!

A mother dog will have a litter of about five or six puppies at the same time. When the puppies are born, they are helpless – they cannot see or hear. They spend most of their first days asleep.

The mother dog will nurse her puppies for about six weeks.

The blind and deaf puppies snuggle up to their littermates for comfort.

The mother licks her new puppies clean.

FACT...

Most Dalmatian puppies are born all white with no spots.

At three weeks puppies begin to stand up.

Growing up

Puppies usually stay with their mother for about eight to ten weeks. By this time they can walk and eat solid food. They are ready to find a new home.

Owners need to give their puppies plenty of attention and affection.

Famous for: having millions of internet fans and his own cuddly toy on sale

Breed: Pomeranian

Owned by: Irene Ahn, San Francisco, USA

Puppies play fight with their brothers and sisters.

Puppies have lots of energy.

Understanding your puppy

It is important to understand your puppy. Your puppy raises or lowers its ears if it is happy or sad. It might growl or thump its tail when cross.

If your puppy lowers its front legs and wags its tail, it wants to play.

When a dog is scared it will put its tail between its legs, flatten its ears and drop its head.

FACT ...

Dogs circle around before going to sleep. In the wild, this was done to flatten the grass to make a more comfortable sleeping place.

Dogs sniff each other to find out about one another.

Training

We train puppies to follow our commands by using rewards and giving praise. This helps to keep them safe both at home and outside.

You can teach your puppy to follow commands such as 'sit', 'stay', 'come' and 'lie down'.

Dogs can show off their training on an agility course at a dog show.

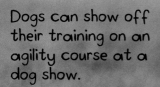

SPOTLIGHT: Jesse the Jack Russell

Famous for: being an internet star who goes shopping and folds the laundry

Breed: Jack Russell

Owned by: Heather Brook, Hollywood, USA

Intelligent dogs can be trained to do tricks – and even surf!

Caring for your dog

Your dog needs lots of affection, attention and a place to sleep; it needs the right food and exercise. It also needs you to check its teeth and general health and organize for it to have the right vaccinations from a vet.

You should groom your dog regularly to keep its fur clean.

Dogs need to have exercise
every day. Working dogs
and gundogs, such
as this retriever,
need long walks.

You need to brush your dog's teeth every day.

GLOSSARY

agility course A series of obstacles for a dog to go through successfully as fast as possible.

breed A group of animals that all look very similar.

communication Telling others what you are thinking or feeling.

domestic Tamed to live safely with humans.

explosives Chemicals that can blow things up.

gundog A type of hunting dog trained to help its owner find and bring back prey.

herding Gathering together a group of animals, such as sheep.

highwayman A person who used to attack stagecoaches to steal money and valuables from travellers.

instinct Knowing without being taught.

intelligent Clever.

lean Thin and strong.

littermates Brother and sister puppies that are born at the same time.

loyal Trusting and friendly.

prey An animal that is hunted by another animal.

service dog A dog that helps people with certain needs.

species A group of animals that look similar and that are all related.

stagecoach A large carriage pulled by horses that carried passengers from place to place.

stamina The ability to exercise for a long time.

tracking Following the trail of something or someone to find it.

vaccination Medicine given to a puppy or dog with a needle and syringe to stop it becoming ill in the future.

INDEX